# Feng Shui Secrets
*for*
# College Students

*by*

# *Nadine Gross*

---

To: ...............................................................

From: ........................................................

*You deserve all the energy you need for all the education, health, love and money you want!*

---

Copyright © 2012 Nadine Gross

All rights reserved.

ISBN-13: 978-1478270508

For Bulk Sales Information
please call (516) 965-0144
or Email FengShuing@Bellsouth.net

## WHY YOU NEED THIS BOOK

Personal Energy - the energy of our mind and body - comes from food and external stimuli such as light, color, sound, touch and smell.

*Feng Shui for College Students* is important because we all live in a "personal space" which directly influences our Personal Energy.

Organizing our personal space into empowered work, study and sleeping spaces helps us empower our life for good grades and a great social life.

Create and own your space with the goal of maximizing your personal energy to insure a successful future.

*Feng Shui Secrets...*

# CONTENTS

| | | |
|---|---|---|
| 1 | My Story | 1 |
| 2 | The Energy Tool | 7 |
| 3 | Elements | 13 |
| 4. | Personal Inner Space | 28 |
| 5. | Outer Spaces | 32 |
| 6. | Personal Energy | 42 |
| 7. | Energy of Buildings | 53 |
| 8. | Classroom Energy | 58 |
| 9. | Energy that Promotes You | 60 |
| 10. | Business Energy | 65 |
| 11. | Health, Wealth & Love | 71 |
| 12. | The Garden Cure | 85 |
| 13. | Your Power | 89 |
| 13. | When Little Aches Bother You | 95 |
| 14. | Chinese Astrology Animals & Colors | 100 |

## ACKNOWLEDGMENTS

Clint, Alison, Rob, Tu, Bill, Minnie and Sara, thank you for your support.

To my friends Susan, Maria, Linda and Jill, thank you for your input.

Thanks to Archie Asher, Student Coordinator of Broward State College, for calling my attention to the fact that not all students live on campus.

# 1
# MY STORY

We all hit crossroads in our lives. These occur precisely at times when all seems bleakest, and during these times personal energy and the energy of the space we occupy are most important.

I graduated from a high school that was close to my home. The neighborhood and my friends were my comfort zone. The surroundings were warm and friendly, and all my childhood friends lived close by.

Friends and family were my support system, and I took them for granted. Everyone was a familiar face attached to a warm greeting.

College was the exciting unknown.

*Feng Shui Secrets...*

My college required freshmen to live on campus in student residences. My building was new and very modern. I found it cold and strange to live in that environment.

To make things worse, my roommate was even stranger. She was rude, she took up the whole room with her stuff spread out everywhere, and she borrowed my clothes without permission. She used my books, my paper, and my notes, and she treated me like I was her servant. Her tone of voice was scornful and harsh.

I tried to move to another space, but nothing was available. I was frustrated and was stuck in a difficult situation.

My grandparents raised me to be polite. I called my grandmother and told her my problem. I could not function in this environment. I was afraid I would fail.

My grandmother advised that I should stand up for my self, be firm, and tell my roommate how I felt. "No is a very important word," she explained. "It sets boundaries. I know this is difficult for you, but you must stop this now." My grandmother was very firm about this.

I went back to the room, sick to my stomach. I was completely intimidated by this person. *How could I stand up to her?* She was a head taller than me, and fifty pounds heavier.

The room was empty when I got back. Thank goodness, she was not there.

I took back everything she borrowed from me. She was such a slob. I spent hours that day cleaning the room to make it look decent.

Her clothes were all over the floor. I put them in a huge pile on her bed, and I put a note on top that read, "This is not a

pigsty. Do not clutter the floor or the room. Do not touch my things or borrow anything without my permission.
- Nadine"

When she returned, she screamed and started to throw her clothes on the floor. She went to my desk, to throw everything on it on the floor, but I intercepted her hand and yelled "Stop!"

To my amazement she did.

"What kind of home did you grow up in?" I asked her. "Where are your manners? I am ashamed of your behavior, and the way you live. You could be a neat, good looking person – why don't you live that way?"

Her answer to me was that this was the way she lived at home, and her mother simply closed her bedroom door and ignored it.

I said, "We have to respect each other and respect our room." It was a small cell containing two beds, two desks, two chests-of-drawers, and two closets.

I suggested that we decorate the room together. We divided the room and defined each half with colors we preferred.

We even coordinated our colors to make the room look larger. We decided on a color theme together, and picked the colors pink and wine (burgundy.)

By working together to make the space look pretty, we claimed the space as our home.

When we worked together, we became friends who respected each other's possessions and space.

When we put aside our differences and made decisions as a team, we respected each other. We could then work and solve problems together, as friends.

# 2

# THE ENERGY TOOL

*"What we are today comes from our thoughts of yesterday, and our present thoughts build out like for tomorrow. Our life is the creation of our mind. "*
  *Gautama Buddha*


Feng Shui is a system that harnesses the earth's energy to create a better life.

On the back cover is a diagram called an Energy Tool. In Chinese it is called a Ba Qua' (pronounced ba kwa). It tells you about which kind of energy corresponds to each area in a room or building.

The door of a room is where energy enters the room; this energy brings a life force into the room when the door is open.

Stand in the open doorway to your room and hold the energy tool in front of you at your waist. This is how you will hold the tool to analyze different areas and energies of a room.

You use the doorway to judge the energy of the room. The door must be able to open a full 90°

Put a picture of trees or a garden by the door to bring about growth in your life. This is a way to train your mind for growth.

Seeing growth trains your mind to accept growth.

When the Life Force is high, the space has a great deal of positive energy. The space feeds you, if the space's energy is high, you will be full of energy.

The door of your room is the career section of your room. Put a poster on the back of the door showing the career path you have chosen. If you are studying medicine, hang a poster showing, doctors at work. The poster will stimulate your mind and your career path.

Put a black mat on the floor inside the door of your room. Black is the color of career. Now you can walk your career path.

Hang a red metal wind chime in the window facing the entrance door of your room. Sound stimulates the mind. The music of the wind chime will stimulate the fame area of your room and your life.

If you do not have a window opposite the door, hang a mobile across from the door. Use shades of red in the mobile. The action of a spinning mobile will empower the fame area of the room.

A balance of career, fame and reputation will jumpstart your career when you graduate, and help give you the opportunity to pursue the career you have chosen. This will also help you get an internship in your chosen field. Feng Shui trains the mind for success.

Once you have done the above simple adjustment to the career and fame area of your room, wait to see and feel the feel the energy change.

## Test If the Energy Has Changed

Put your hands parallel to the floor and feel how the energy feels on both palms of your hands before you make the changes and after you make the changes. The room should feel more balanced. Trust your intuition.

As you feel the energy change, it will feel comfortable and settled.

Balance the energy and it will open the path of success for you.

It is time for the next adjustment of your

space. Walk through your space and try to notice any area that does not feel right. You can change the area in the following ways:

1. Locate the color box for a given space in your room on the Energy Tool, and do whatever you can to add, feature, or enhance that color in that area of the room.

2. Clean up the clutter.

3. Add light, a plant, a mirror or a crystal to the space.

Remember that it is important to balance the space by doing small corrections in the opposite corner of the room. For example:

Career is the black box, while Fame is the red box. They balance each other.

(Career is your chosen path of work, and fame is your reputation as an excellent student in your chosen field. The good job you did on your internship will provide you with a letter of recommendation or a job offer when you graduate.

Check the Energy Tool.

| BOX | COLOR |
|---|---|
| 1. Career | black |
| 2. Relationship | pink |
| 3. New Beginnings | green |
| 4. Wealth | purple |
| 5. Good Fortune | yellow |
| 6. Helpful People | grey |
| 7. Creativity | white |
| 8. Knowledge | blue/green |
| 9. Fame | red |

# 3

# ELEMENTS

1. **Career**: The element that relates to Career is water. Put a water fountain by your front door to enhance your career studies and prospects.

Water is also communication, so your front door must open a full 90°, in order for you to have complete communication power. Put a picture of growth on the back of the door, such as a picture of a forest. When you see growth, you are training the mind that it must grow.

I once had a client who complained to me that she was loosing her hearing in the right ear. I showed her that each part of the color box is related to a part of the body, and that the front door controls the ear. I opened her front door and because she had a closet behind the door with a hook on the closet to hang coats, she could not open the front door a full 90°.

When I asked her what was in the closet she replied, "Do not open the closet."

When I opened the closet all kinds of junk fell out. She could not remember the last time she used any of it. We put all the junk in large plastic bags and cleared the closet. We recycled everything, including the hook, to Goodwill. It was hard for her to believe her hearing would improve, but within a few months her hearing was restored. (As a native New Yorker, to me the best part of it all was that she gained a closet).

2. **Relationship** is an earth element, so you should put a nice plant in your relationship area to keep your relationships grounded and growing. The

color of relationship is Pink. The part of the body it controls is the abdomen. Clutter in that area will cause stomach problems.

Ladies, use pink sheets to have a romantic relationship. For passion, wrap the bed in red fabric, then put on the pink sheets. Paint your bedroom pink.

Men can paint the bedroom a light green for new beginnings and the wall behind your bed a deep wine color. To encourage a perfect relationship, men can use dark wine sheets with either a stripe or plaid with a touch of pink, wine or green for new beginning. If you cannot paint your walls, use wall hangings or pictures with the advised colors in them.

I invited a friend to come to Florida and visit. She had just been through a bad time with breast cancer and needed a change of scenery.

When she arrived, she told me her boyfriend of many years hasd left her for a younger, healthier woman. She was devastated. I put pink sheets on the bed in the guest room. I sent her down to the pool to read a book and relax. She met a single man from the next building at the pool. When she left, the romance followed her. Six months later, he proposed and she moved in with him. They have lived happily, together, ever after.

## <u>A Relationship Wish Tray</u>

To make a relationship-wish tray, find a mirror in the shape of a square. Place a picture on it of the type of person you want to be with. On a sheet of paper, write down the qualities you want them to have. Paste that list of qualities on the back of the picture. Attach a single rose to the picture, to make your life smell like a rose.

Burn a pink candle in the relationship corner to develop a relationship. Burn the candle or an electric candle a few minutes each day and watch your dreams unfold.

3. **Family and New Beginnings** are represented by the element of wood, and the corresponding color is green.

If you haven't heard from your family, take out all the old pictures, frame them in interesting frames, paint the wall green, and hang up all the pictures on the green wall.

One of my clients painted the wall dark green and all the frames white. She hung the pictures in this order: her wedding picture, pictures of her children, and then pictures of her grandchildren.

Then she called her oldest son and opened the door to renew the relationship. Now if you try to phone her you can never find her at home — she is constantly traveling to see her seven children and 27 grandchildren!

You must create an energy that brings your family to you.

Be creative, and if you want to bring people into your life, you hang up pictures of the people you want in your life.

To bring about new beginnings, employ the color green. Burn a pink candle, and a green candle to reinforce your intention.

4. **Health & Wealth** correspond to the color purple, which is also a wood element.

Health is most important, so be sure to paint that space a shade of purple and put wood furniture in it.

Hold the Energy Tool at your waist, (orienting the black box closest to your waist) and stand at your front door. The purple box shows you your money corner.

The purple box should be the master bedroom, because it is the power corner of the house. Vote for a house leader, that person should occupy the power corner of the house. His or her roommate should be second in command. They are responsible for the condition of the house and the good will of all those living there.

If the power area is your kitchen, have a purple, lavender or mauve painted wall. Place a purple mat by the sink and include purple accessories. Color empowers.

One client hung a purple picture frame with money from all over the world. She is an international agent for syndication and licensing. She put this in the money corner of her kitchen and the money keeps flowing in.

5. **Good Fortune** correlates to the color yellow, and is an earth element.

If you have a wall blocking the center of your space, put a mirror on both sides of the wall to create a window in the wall.

I like to use round porthole mirrors. The

round shape represents heaven, and the square of a wall is the shape of earth. The round mirror creates heaven on earth.

Remember to keep the center of your space open to let the space breathe. Good Fortune is the center of the Energy Tool, represented by the yellow color box.

6. **Helpful People** are in the Heaven section of your space, and this area is related to metal elements, especially soft metals like bronze, copper and lead. It is the grey color box.

Metal helps with diplomatic communication.

Heaven is a perfect area for a home office, library, or study room. Work done from this area makes it easier to achieve your goals. If your front door is located in this area, you have no trouble getting help.

Not long ago one of my clients called me in a panic, "I lost my job today," she told me. "I invited all my family to my house for Thanksgiving. What am I to do? If I make the dinner, I will not have enough money to pay my bills. I invited twenty people."

I told her to put a plant by the door in the helpful people corner. To balance the helpful people (grey box) she put three coins tied together with red string in the money corner of the house.

Soon after, a friend of hers called to tell my client that she was pregnant. She asked for maternity leave and wanted to know if my client would do her a favor and take over her job until she was able to come back to work.

My client contacted the firm and interviewed for the job. She was hired and she started the day after Thanksgiving.


**7. Creativity and Children:** The metal element of this white box is represented by hard metal, like steel. Do your creative work in this area and you will cut through your difficulties like a sharp blade through soft wood. Writers, artists, architects, and lawyers find this position to their advantage.

A writer I knew complained of being blocked. He had published one novel and owed his publisher the second novel of a trilogy.

He moved into a new space that had a stone courtyard in the creative (white box) area. We put planters in the courtyard and filled them with all the colors of the five elements.

1. Purple flowers in the Wealth area.

2. Red flowers, in the Fame area of the courtyard.

3. Pink flowers in the Relationship area.

4. White flowers in creativity.

The stones in the courtyard correspond to the 5th color zone, Grey, for the Heaven to Earth element.

6. Black planter boxes.

7. A large indoor - outdoor carpet was placed in the center of the courtyard. The colors of the carpet were, blue, green, to represent the wood element and gold color is an earth element, which completed the five elements, creating all the colors of the Energy Tool color box, and balanced the courtyard.

The changes were drastic. He claimed

the ideas flowed and he just kept writing until he finished the second book.

**8. Knowledge & Self-Cultivation:** The turquoise box is the last of the earth sections. This is symbolic of a mountain. This area of a room, house or building makes a wonderful library, den, or workout space.

The knowledge and self cultivation area is the best place in your room for meditation or studying. If possible, place your desk in this area.

A mother of two small boys called me to consult on their rooms. They were not doing well in school and could not seem to be able to sit and concentrate.

We moved their desks in their bedrooms to the Knowledge corner of the room. They went from just passing their exams, to getting A's.

9. **Fame and Reputation**: The fire element of this red box controls your fame and reputation. If you want to run for office or be known for a special talent, empower this area with the color red and you will be on your way to becoming famous.

A student wanted to run for office in his school. He wanted to show leadership but was very shy.

"I need this for college," he told me. "They want leaders. What should I do?"

"What are you good at?" I asked.

"My best subject is math."

"Run for treasurer of your school," I replied. "That position is not an easy one, but you are skilled in math and that is the skill you need for that job."

We put his picture in the fame area of

his bedroom and put a banner across the picture reading *Class Teasurer*. The intention inspired him to reach out to his friends for support in this endeavor. They did what he requested and sure enough, he won the position.

Note the colors and their position on the color chart. If you are allowed to paint the space a shade of that color, you will enhance the power of the space to actualize your dreams, goals, and ambitions as they relate to each area of your room.

# 4

# PERSONAL INNER SPACE

$E=MC^2$
*(Energy= Motivation, Courage, Change)*

The key to life is Energy, and this book teaches you how to keep your energy at an all time high.

Our eyes are stimulated by color, movement, and light. The brain receives messages from the eyes, and motivates us to change our energy.

Color and light add energy to a space, and the space in turn feeds you the energy you need.

You can add movement using wind chimes, a fish tank with live fish, mobiles, clocks with hands that move, (broken clocks should be repaired or thrown out) or fluttering ribbons tied to an air conditioner to supply movement.

If you don't have energy you cannot stay motivated. Students start projects and burn out before they finish. This is caused by negative energy that drains the student and takes away their motivation.

Feng Shui keeps the energy positive so you can finish your work.

To effect change in areas of your life that need improvement, you must have courage to change what is known, even when that change becomes uncomfortable and does not feel as if it is working for you.

Without change there is no growth. In life, we grow or we die. By using color and light, placing our possessions with intention, and with the use of the Energy Tool, you can un-clutter, change colors appropriately, and empower the spaces in your life to make changes for the better.

Personal Space is your inner space, heart, mind and body.

Make a list of the areas in your life you want to improve.

You can place the Energy Tool over your body. If you feel a part of the body is not functioning as it should, look to the space in your room or home that relates to that body part.

1. Is the space cluttered? If so clear the space.

2. Wear green underwear to heal that part of the body.

Even the food on your plate should represent all the colors of the spectrum, including green, yellow, red, purple, white and black or dark brown. You can find all of these colors in vegetables and fruits. Meat is brown, chicken and fish are the white foods. Vegetables, fruits and meats, represent all the mineral elements required by your body.

Remember that it takes courage to stick with changes even when they feel uncomfortable. It takes time to change, so have patience.

Stay motivated; if you feel you are going into a slump, analyze your space and make the necessary energy corrections.

Use the Energy Tool to define each area. Check the space for clutter,. Move your possessions until the space feels open and balanced.

Use the formula of this chapter to keep you mindful that Feng Shui is an ongoing process of adjustments to energy in the form of color, light, and your personal belongings.

# 5

# OUTER SPACES

When we leave the comforts of our personal space, outside spaces impact our lives.

If the neighborhood we live in is transitional and everyone is fixing up their homes, caring for their lawns, planting flowers, fixing the sidewalks, and painting their houses, we feel good about the outside space that surrounds us.

However, if the neighborhood is deteriorating, if windows are broken, cars are abandoned, garbage cans are left in the street, and street lights are broken, it is time to call a neighborhood committee together to preserve the value of your investment in your home. Or it might be time to move.

The later environment is negative and will eventually impact on how you feel about yourself. If your neighborhood is failing, your brain tells you that you are failing. That will impact on your personal and professional life. Where you live and your surroundings tells your brain that you are a success or a failure.

It is not advisable to live in a basement. Underground energy is not the best energy to live or work in.

If your space is underground, put up posters, or artwork of gardens and growth.

A grass-green rug will help give an outdoor illusion, to the space. Keep the area warm and dry, use a heater and a dehumidifier to ward off dampness and mold, which will make you sick. The next step is to move above ground level.

Take time each day to be outside in the

fresh air. Look at nature or walk in the park. Take a deep breath and relax. Go on a mini-vacation to refresh yourself and your brain. The day will not seem as long and you will not be as tired when you get home.

When looking for a job, try to find work in an area that feels comfortable and has pleasant surroundings. If the building you work in is in an area that has a welcoming feeling about it, you will feel better about coming to work each day.

Outer spaces impact heavily upon our emotions. If the view is beautiful, we feel better about ourselves. A walk in a park with trees and grass will energize you.

Real estate agents say an area must have three things to make it valuable.

1. Location
2. Location
3. Location

Put yourself in the best location!

If you can have a plant or two in your workspace, by all means do it. Plants keep us healthy. Open the windows, if you can, to air out your space and bring in clean air. If you are in an air-conditioned space, bring in an air purifier to help you stay well.

Look at the Energy Tool. Note the colors on the boxes and paint each space a shade of that color to enhance the harmony of the space. Remember the black box is at your waist and the door is the mouth of the room — that is how the area energizes.

Look at both sides of the street where you live. If your house is the smallest house on the street you can raise the energy of the house with lighting.

Paint your house a different color from the rest of the houses in the area. Accent the special features of the house with another shade of the main house color or with an accent color.

Paint stores have staff and brochures that will show you how to pick accent colors.

Paint your door and window trim, shutters, porch, and window boxes a different color of the house or a darker or lighter color, to make these features stand out. Now the energy of your home will be stronger than just a boring plain beige or white house without accented trim.

If your house is the largest house on the street, you do not want it to stand out as an unfriendly structure among smaller less important structures. The color of this house should be a neutral one, because the structure is so grand. Plants around the house will soften the lines and make it friendly to the neighborhood.

## Store Fronts

Many of you will work in the retail field, and some of you will open your own retail businesses.

A corner store needs a revolving door to bring in business. You will increase the traffic flow to your commercial space through the revolving door energy.

If your business is down from the corner, have the door open to the flow of traffic on your side of the street. An open door will bring in more traffic when it is in harmony with the flow of pedestrian traffic as well as the flow of auto traffic.

Highway traffic is always a concern in both commercial and residential areas. Trees and high bushes will muffle the noise. Double pane windows can also control noise, and they have a side benefit of improving the insulation of your building.

If you have a commercial building, always make sure the front door faces the road. It is a welcoming energy factor. A side door on commercial buildings is hard to find and the energy is strange and un-welcoming. This type of building will rent slower than a building with an entrance facing the street.

Signage should always face the heavy traffic flow to energize business. Use contrasting bright colors on signs. Black represents communication, and red indicates action. Think of a fast food chain like McDonald's; their signage and branding uses *red* (fire, element and fame), *black* (communication,) and *white* (creativity) to move the customer in and out quickly. Turnover is a critical key to fast food restaurants. Bright lights together with bright hot colors make people want to eat quickly and get back to work.

Restaurants that specialize in fine dining do not use bright and hot colors. They use earth tones to ground the customers, soft blues and greens, and soft lighting to create a romantic ambiance. The customer wants to dine and relax in those colors.

Notice that some stores use colored signs and paint the walls the same color of the sign to make the different areas of merchandise easy to identify. You can find what you are looking for just by color code and matching signage. These stores are easier and more comfortable to shop in than stores that are all one color.

Buildings that are painted all one color are very hard to navigate. For example, buildings on campus are often all the same color., and strangers to the campus get lost even if good signage is present.

Color is the strongest motivator and space definition indicator we have.

1. What color is a building?

2. The color of the signage should work with the color of the building and the street.

3. Note the traffic flow. In a large development, color can direct the traffic to your door.

4. Use color to direct traffic and define spaces. Color defining spaces and buildings create an inexpensive visual method of directing traffic, especially when you couple it with the use of proper signage.

When you accept a position with a company, notice the condition of the street and the position of the space or store on that street.

Never work in a store with dirty windows. The life force of the store is not in good health, and the store will soon close.

# 6

# PERSONAL ENERGY

Do You Meditate?

Meditation helps you to center yourself and create balance in you life.

Center yourself by imagining a line going down the center of your body. Start at the top of your head and draw that line down to your feet. Imagine that line as your energy line. Feel the energy radiating out through your body until it feels warm and relaxed.

If you didn't sleep well last night, this will create the feeling of a good night's sleep.

A quiet moment just before you go to sleep or when you wake up is a perfect time to meditate.

Meditation sets the tone for the day or night.

What is your favorite destination? It can be a vacation spot, fishing hole, surfing beach, golf outing, a hike in the mountains, or a canoe trip down a lazy stream.

Get your favorite meditation CD music playing softly and sit yourself in a comfortable position, wearing comfortable attire. Position your hands on your knees, touch your thumbs to your fore fingers, and allow yourself to relax.

Close your eyes and go to your special place. Quiet your mind, and if your mind starts to wander or think about stuff, acknowledge it and say, "I will do that later," then try to quiet your mind again.

*Feng Shui Secrets...*

Think of your mind as a large blackboard and erase all thoughts. Set aside enough time to give yourself a deep meditation.

Try to wake up 15 minutes earlier in the morning. Do the morning meditation right after you awake. Allow 15 minutes at night to meditate, and this will help you achieve a better night's rest.

As you practice meditation, you will be able to do it in less time and get the same results. Have a special place to meditate, block the area off with a screen, have a scented candle, a spiritual figurine or picture. A corner in your bedroom would be perfect.

The **Bedroom** is one of the most important rooms in your life because that is where your sleep. When you are asleep, the subconscious works for you.

Unblock all cluttered corners and bedroom closet. Do not have cluttered counter tops. If you have a TV in the bedroom, cover it with natural fibre or wood. A cotton shawl cuts the radiation of the TV so it does not affect your resting energy.

Your bed should not be under a window. If that is the only wall on which you can position your bed, cover the windows with drapery, shutters, or shades. When you sleep, the window's covers should be closed to keep the energy from flying out the window.

Your bed should not be on a water wall (bathroom wall). If it is on a water wall, cover the bedroom wall with a quilt for decoration and to block the energy of the water.

Your bathroom door should not cut across the bed. If it does, hang a 20mm crystal ball on a red string in the center of the bathroom door, hanging so that the crystal is clear of the doorframe and gets light. The light it throws forms a rainbow in the crystal, dispersing the light sideways, away from the bed. Keep the bathroom door closed. A mirror on the bedroom side of a bathroom door reflects the sewage energy away.

You should not have a fan over your bed. The fan has blades which act as swords over the area it covers.

If you do have a fan over the bed, the cure is to place colored dots on top of the blades, (when you place them on top of the fan blades, no one knows they're there) the colored dots on the fan blades should represent the 5 elements, and say a prayer of your choice nine times. The fan is now a prayer wheel.

The colors of the dots are as follows:

1. *Blue and green* for wood (place blue and green on the same blade).

2. *Red* for fire (you can't have a fire without wood.)

3. *Yellow* for earth (ash of fire makes earth.)

4. *White* for metal (compress earth and it makes ore which becomes metal.)

5. *Black* for water (metal when it is cold condenses into water.)

This creates a positive cycle when you turn on the fan.

If you only have 4 blades put *black* and *white* together on the same blade.

**Bathroom**: is a water element. To stop floods, use the color red for the shower curtain, towels and accessories. Red is the color of fire. Fire boils off water. The other colors you can use are earth colors, brown, yellow, terra cotta, beige; they are earth colors, earth dams water.

Always keep your toilet seat down to make sure the sewage energy is covered. If this is not possible, put a mirror above the toilet, mirror side facing down, to reflect the downward flow of energy back up into the room.

**Kitchen**: You should not be able to see the stove from the front door. Many kitchens are in the front of an apartment or house. To see the stove from the front door causes fires.

The simple cure is to cover the burners so they look like part of the counter. Have a wall blocking the entrance to the kitchen or close a door between the kitchen and front hall. A simple folding screen could be put up to block the view.

I pointed out the danger of the stove and front door relationship to a client in Levittown, New York. She did not feel this was important, and left the stove visible from the front door. The fire department called her at work to report her home had burnt to the ground.

I am glad my other clients have taken this warning seriously.

### Family Placement for Harmony

When selecting a bedroom, the astrology of each person is important. Look at the Energy Tool, color boxes, and check the astrology of each person.

Purple is the power corner of the house, and this should be the Master Suite. Students living in a group housing situation should elect a leader of their house. That is the purple position. The leader gets that power position. *The snake and the dragon astrology animals have this position.*

A middle daughter's bedroom is in the

red or fame area. *The horse is in this position.* The horse holds the fame position, and the color of that box red.

The master bedroom can be in the pink area that is relationship. *The ram and the monkey share this position.*

The youngest daughter's bedroom is the white area (creativity). *The rooster has this position.*

If a parent is living with you, place them in the grey area, heaven, and helpful people, so they are appreciated as the grandparent in the house. The most likely person to help everyone gets this space. *The dog and the pig are in this position.*

Black is the area for the middle son (communication and career). *The rat owns this space.* If the door enters in the center of the house, people living there are career minded.

Turquoise is the area for the youngest son (knowledge). *The tiger and the ox share the knowledge position.*

Green is the area for the oldest son, (family and new beginnings). *The rabbit holds the new beginnings position.*

If the rooms have already been assigned and a person does not want to change rooms, use the color in the Energy Tool to bring the proper energy into the various spaces. Claim the room by using color and light make to it appropriate to your own astrology, position in the social hierarchy, career and relationship goals.

Summary:

1. Which role describes your function in a group living situation?

2. If you are the youngest daughter in your family or the creative person in the group, the creative space in the house

should be yours. If it is not available paint the room white for creativity.

3. Check your astrology for your astrological animal.

4. Check the placement of your major subject on the Energy Tool. What is the color that represents that major? Then chose the placement of your room in the house or the color for your room.

# 7
# ENERGY OF BUILDINGS

Goals of this chapter:

1. Raise the energy of your learning space.

2. Retain more of what you study and get better grades.

The ideal placements for the following studies are listed below. Each campus is developed by their design plan and architectural codes, and the school may not necessarily have used Feng Shui in determining the placement of the buildings on campus. However, the buildings could be painted the colors that would enhance the energy and make it easier to locate, if the college administration so desired.

By using the color boxes listed on the

Energy Tool, the energy of each building could be raised, and the percentage of students graduating would be much higher.

Start at the front of your building, or the main entrance of the campus.

1. Where is your room located in the building?

2. What is your future profession?

A business college or department should be in the wealth corner of the building. Anything to do with financial matters belongs in the wealth corner. This is the southeast location of the campus from the main entrance. *(Buy a small compass and stand at the main entrance of the campus to find the southeast location.)*

Acting and all stage and screen related courses are in the red (fame) box, located in south corner of the campus from the main entrance.

Social Work, Physiology, Nursing schools can be placed in the nurturing, relationship oriented, and pink box of the Energy Tool which is southwest corner of the campus from the main entrance.

The advertising and art, communications and architecture departments belong in the creative area of the campus.   Find the white Box on the Energy Tool, it will be the west corner of the campus that is the creative area.

The theology college belongs in the grey box, (helpful people, heaven).  Northwest corner from the main entrance would be the proper place for the study of theology.

Anthropology, history, literature, archaeology, palaeontology colleges, belong in the north corner from the main entrance of the university, it is black box on the back cover of this book.

The library, law school, and legal studies, are located in the blue/green box, in the northeast corner of the campus.

Science's and medicine colleges will be best located in the green area (new beginnings). East corner of the campus is the ideal location for science and medicine.

The yellow area (central energy) is a good space for all administrative functions of the university or college.

The above would be the ideal layout for campus buildings. The use of color can correct placement issues, and through color usage, the percentage of graduates from these buildings will increase each term. Feng Shui principles are truly amazing when practiced.

1. Where are you located on the campus?

2. Which buildings do you use?

3. What are the directions of the buildings, north (black), northeast (purple), east (green), south (black), southwest (turquoise), west (white), northwest (pink), southwest (grey), and how do they correspond with your field of study?

4. How does your astrological sign fit in the layout of these buildings?

**Example of a quick cure:**

Cover your books in the color of the subjects. As you color code your subjects, you will automatically select the subject you need to work on the most and apply yourself with extra effort to get better grades.

# 8

## Classroom Energy

You can change the Energy of your classroom so that you get better grades.

Offer to help your professor decorate the classroom. When you put your energy into a space you own that space and it will work for you. You will make better grades in a room that holds your energy.

If the classroom is not dedicated to a single professor but assigned to different professors at different times of the day or week, you can offer to help the professor decorate or arrange their office.

When the professor is comfortable and successful in their office, their perception of you and your help will ingratiate them toward you.

Also, when you help a professor with

their projects, he or she becomes your mentor. When you need a letter of recommendation for a job or graduate school, the professor you help will be the one to help you.

Summary:

1. Find a Mentor

2. Use the Energy Tool to help your mentor.

3. List the ways you can be an asset to your mentor.

4. Ask for letters of recommendation from your professors.

5. If you are able to help your professor decorate your classroom or their office, use the Energy Tool's color boxes to guide you in raising the energy of that space.

# 9

## ENERGY THAT PROMOTES YOU

Did you ever realize, when you decide to find employment or start a business, it feels as if everyone else is doing the same thing?

A student asked me, "How can I get the internship or summer job I want?"

My youngest son graduated Architecture School with a Masters degree, when the economy was at an all time low, building construction was at a halt. He was depressed that the job market was nonexistent, and felt he wasted five years in college.

I reminded him there were part-time

agencies in every field. He signed up with an agency specializing in the field of architecture. We made up a sign listing the agency's name and put the sign facing into a mirror in his bedroom. We wrote "hired" on the back of the sign. The following Monday he was hired. The part time job lasted a year and a half.

He held many jobs during that recession. The economy recovered and all that experience landed him a job with a top architectural firm.

Never give up on your dream! Use Feng Shui energy cures that can help you achieve your goals. Stay focused on what you love to do, use the energy adjustments, and watch life open up and your dreams become reality.

Empower the purple corner of your

room. Make a list of what you would bring to the job you want, face the list in front of a mirror located in your bedroom (the list should be reflected in the mirror), and you will get the job.

You can <u>e-mail</u> or telephone me with your questions.

**fengshuing@bellsouth.net**

Cell: 516-965-0144

## Exercise: Empower Your Bedroom

1. Find the power corner. Make a wish board and put it in that purple corner.

2. Do a layout on this page of how you feel the colors of the room should block out.

3. Keep a record of the areas you put your energy in to.

4. Then ask yourself are you doing better in those classes?

Keep adjusting the energy of your room to keep the desired changes flowing in your life.

As you make adjustments to your room do not forget to make note of them on your drawing and to list the changes in your life in a diary or on your calendar.

Summary:

1. Keep a record of your desires and the

adjustments you made to accomplish the tasks.

2. Did you get better grades?

3. Are you having a better social life?

4. Did you find that special mentor?

5. Do you have a partner?

6. Are you getting an internship?

# 10

# BUSINESS ENERGY

A college student asked me, "Could Feng Shui put me in a business I can do while I am in school? I have several ideas, but I can't seem to get started," he told me. "School takes a lot of my time, I need money, and I can't figure out how to do both. I have to do something. My father lost his job. Things are bad at home. I can't earn enough over the summer and spring break to pay my tuition. I want to stay in college and graduate. I have to balance work with my classes and study, so do you have any ideas about something I can do that's not too demanding? I have to study hard to get good grades?"

He was carrying a full program in computer sciences. We made a list of chores that he had to do for himself. Laundry was first on the list. I suggested he do laundry for other students in the residence at the same time that he did his own.

He went to a laundry facility that had 30 machines. He made a deal with the owner to use all machines at 5:00 AM to 6:00 in the morning, before the facility was officially open.

He contracted with 18 students to do their laundry for $3.00 a bag. The average student had two bags of laundry.

While the laundry was washing he could study, do homework, or take care of making out the bill for each of his client-students.

The first week he netted $50 for a morning's work. The business grew; he contracted for more time with the owner of the laundry.

He worked 5 days a week, hired a helper, and still only worked from 5 AM to 6 AM earning $300 a week. This paid for his helper, the cost of soap, water softener, washing machines and dryers.

I did a special rice blessing on his Residence Room and hung ceremonial firecrackers over the door. (The firecracker cure brings recognition to the person occupying the room and stimulates business.)

We put a plant in the helpful people corner to grow the business. We hung money coins in the money corner of the room.

I told him to a take a picture of the finished laundry bags and hang a poster that said "Laundry Service $3.00 a bag" in all the fraternity houses. His girl-friend put notices up in the sorority houses and joined him.

They maintained a grade point average of 3.5. When they graduated they sold the business to their helpers.

Exercise:

1. Make a list of services you could provide and still have time to study.

2. Pick one service and add up the costs of doing business.

For Example:

a. Travel expenses: gas for your car.

b. Advertising expenses: brochures, business cards, flyers.

c. Cost of Help? Will you need help?

Now add up the cost of your service.

Example: $20 an hour for a tutoring service.

1. Can you tutor a group?

2. How many people can you tutor effectively?

3. How much can you charge per person?

4. If you charge $10 per person and you can effectively tutor five people in an hour, you will earn $50 for the hour.

5. Can you tutor more than one day?

6. How many days can you tutor and keep up with your work?

7. If you have an assistant, and can tutor ten people together, you will ear $100 for the hour. If you pay the assistant $25 for the hour you will earn $75 per hour.

8. What can you earn in a week?

Once you establish your business plan, put it into action. Make a flyer. Get the news out on campus. Establish a calendar. It is most important that you are reliable and prompt. Time is how you make your money. Respect your time and that of others.

# 11
# HEALTH, WEALTH & LOVE

The goal of this chapter is to teach you how to use Feng Shui to improve your health, wealth, and love-life.

## Health:

Most people are concerned with their health today. Our foods are not pure. They contain hormones and antibiotics, Cows don't graze like they use to, they are fed fillers and we do not know what is in them. Chickens are treated the same way. Vegetables have pesticides unless organically grown.

We are getting fat, but not healthy. Our lifestyle does not make us exercise like we did when we were farmers. As farmers we exercised, our work was manual labor. We no longer farm – we sit.

The chapter on your Personal Inner Space talks about the color of your food. Vegetables and fruits have different colors. Each, vegetables has a different mineral value. Use Feng Shui color theory in your foods to balance the minerals in your body.

How we place our bed is critical to our rest. The optimal direction of the headboard depends on your personal astrology. The person's astrology direction determines how comfortably they will sleep. The headboard should separate your bed from the wall. See the Astrology chart on the following pages.

Buy a Boy Scout compass to determine direction. Look up your sign by year in the back of the book. Determine the direction of your headboard. Move it if you can. If not, use a mirror to reflect the direction your headboard to the proper wall.

The walls in the bedroom have electrical energy for bedroom lighting placed inside the wall. The bed has metal springs and a metal frame - both conduct electricity. The headboard should be wood - wood does not conduct electricity.

The human body has an electrical current, and the metal in the box spring and mattress can throw off the natural electricity of our body. This will make you feel tired.

Use a headboard made of wood. You can buy two quilts and make your own headboard out of one quilt. Buy a piece of plywood. Staple one quilt to the plywood and use the other quilt on your bed. The quilted headboard is very comfortable to lean against. The matching quilts give the room a decorator look. This headboard will stop electricity. You must use natural fibers such as cotton, wool, linen, silk or flax, not polyester.

## Direction of the Head Board Wall Using Chinese Astrological Signs

| | | |
|---|---|---|
| South wall | red | Horse |
| Southwest | pink | Ram/Monkey |
| West wall | white | Rooster |
| Northwest wall | grey | Dog/Pig |
| North wall | black | Rat |
| Northeast | turquoise | Ox/Tiger |
| East wall | green | Rabbit |
| Southeast | purple | Dragon/Snake |

If you have an ailment, look at the

Energy Tool on the back cover, for the part of the body that is giving you a problem. Use *Black* as the front door of the space, locate that area in your space, clear the problem of the space and cure your illness.

Find out the history of a space before you rent or buy it. You can ask the neighbors about the people who lived in the house. If it has a bad history, try these cures. Open the front and back door of the house, or front door and back window, of the apartment, and circulate fresh air throughout the space. Burn incense or sage and bang pot lids together to raise the energy of the space and cure it.

Make sure the sage smoke and the noise of the banging pot lids cover every corner of the space from attic to basement.

Some spaces cannot be cured. Buildings built on a cemetery cannot be cured.

Spaces near a cemetery can have problems. Spirits that are not at rest could attack your space. If you are in a space that just does not feel right, leave immediately. Do not occupy a space that has problems. There is always someplace else, so keep looking.

If a house faces a cemetery, you can have the landlord plant high bushes on the side that faces the cemetery. Block your view of the cemetery with healthy growing bushes and trees.

Do not buy or rent a house with a road facing the house forming a "T". The road is a hidden arrow that will bring illness and ill fortune to the house.

It can be cured by placing an eight sided red ba qua' mirror on your front door facing the road. You can buy this in a

Chinese Store or from me.

Give these cures nine weeks to work. If they do not work, call in a space-clearing professional or call me for help. *(You can find my phone number in the back of the book)*

## A House on a Cul de Sac

If there is illness in the first house on a cul de sac, it will spread to the next house. Soon the cul de sac will be occupied entirely by sick people.

The simple cure is to plant tall hedges between the houses. Plants stop illness. Healthy plants and healthy gardens keep the house healthy and its occupants healthy.

## Wealth

What is Wealth?

Some people feel friends are wealth. If that describes your outlook on life, look to the relationship pink box in the Energy Tool, and empower that corner of your space with pictures of your friends or a picture of the type of people you would like as friends.

<u>If money means wealth for you, here are three easy cures for money.</u>

1. Buy a piggy bank (it must be a new one,.) Put a small mirror on the top of the bank, tape the mirror side facing into the bank. Put a matching small mirror on the bottom of the bank facing in to the bank. Wrap the Piggy bank with the two mirrors taped top and bottom in a red silk or red natural fiber cloth.

Then purchase something or break a bill so that you get new change. You must use new change every day for nine days. The coins you put in the bank must be the same denomination. The money must be new to you.

The larger the denomination the better it will work. (I use quarter because it is easy to get a new roll of quarters from z bank every day for the nine days.) You can continue this in increments of nine days, (for example 9, 18, 27 days) until the money opportunities flow in.

2. Get a red string that is 9 inches long with 3 Chinese coins on it, hang the red string with the 3 Chinese coins on your front door knob, inside the house, and watch the money flow in.

3. Do a Rice Blessing and keep a red envelop filled with the blessed rice in

your wallet, and you will always have money.

## How to do a Rice Blessing

Mix a teaspoon of cinnamon, brown sugar, and paprika into a cup of uncooked rice. Mix all these ingredients with ten capfuls of high proof liquor. Only use this liquor for the rice blessings; it is not to be ingested.

A small size Vodka bottle like the bottles used on airplanes is perfect and inexpensive.

Mix this ninety times with your index finger of your right hand for females and the left hand index finger for males.

Sprinkle the Blessed Rice in the four corners of your room.

Seal the door by putting the rice mixture in the center of the doorframe, top and bottom, and the top and bottom of the sides of the doorframe. You will have six seals on the door when you are finished. Seal all doors that lead out side on the ground floor.

Seal the toilet to keep money from going down the drain by putting a few grains of the Blessed Rice in the toilet.

The rice blessing seals all the good into your space and keeps the negative energy out.

## LOVE

Color is a great energy motivator. All shades of Pink are the color of relationship.

What do you have in your bedroom that says love?

If you have a poster of a Rock Band all that says is you love that band.

You should have a picture of a couple embracing. That shows love between two people, it trains your mind to open your heart for love.

Put a mirror tray on a night table in the love corner of the room, with a crystal lamp to light the corner and crystallize your intentions.

Put a picture of the type of person you wish to attract.

Put a pink scented candle and light it a few minutes each night to bring in the love you deserve.

A picture of the rings you will exchange on that special day.

A brochure of where you and your mate will honeymoon. All this should be on the tray.

*Remember: That special person will not fall out of the sky. You must make an effort to be socially active. Go out with friends to places where you can meet your soulmate.

Put a red carpet in the front hall of your living space, walk over the red carpet and get red carpet treatment wherever you go.

I have a client who lives in a very rural area in the south. She is a high school teacher. "How will I ever meet a man in this lonely part of the country?" She asked me. I suggested that she try the Feng Shui energy cures and see what happened. I made a special trip to her home and we worked together to change the energy. The space felt better when I left.

Two weeks later, a deliveryman from FedEx brought her a package. He was young, good looking, single, and asked her out on a date. They are still together.

I guess you never know how love will come into your life.

*Change your energy*

*and change your destiny.*

Catalog your progress:

List all the foods you eat. List the foods you are missing in you diet. Put a list of foods that are easy for you to add to your diet that will keep you healthy.

Example:

1. Fruits – apples, oranges, melons in season.

2. Vegetables – broccoli, carrots, tomatoes, etc.

3. Fish, Meat, Poultry

## 12

## THE GARDEN CURE

Many students live at home and have asked me about the land around their home. Could the land improve conditions in the home? Could the land help the family?

*This cure is the simplest of all!*

Put the Energy Tool over a diagram of your land. If it is square or rectangular this is an easy cure.

If you have an odd shaped lot there is a way to handle the outside energy working with the land's shape.

If you introduce plants, light, water, sculpture, stones, gravel and trees with intention of giving the odd shaped land back to nature and her spirits, you can "square off" the land.

The land feeds the house and the house feeds you, keeping your energy high.

Plant a money tree, Lilacs (purple,) in the left hand corner of your back yard. Place red flowers across the back on the fame area. A trellis with climbing Bougainvillea grows quickly and would beautify the space. Go to a garden center and they will help you find the right plants for your region.

The relationship corner is pink and should have pink flowers. Roses come in several shades of pink to add interest and energy to the Love area. Put a love seat in the romance corner.

A house on a Cul de Sac may have land that is narrow in front and wide in back. This is called the Money purse. Money goes in but does not come out. Plant the colors of the Energy Color Chart as stated above. This is the most auspicious space, as it has extensions in Money and Love.

A curved road does the opposite — the front is larger than the back causing a loss of space in Money and Love. The small back forms a dustpan shape, so money comes in but is swept out just as fast.

I have found many homes in foreclosure fit this shape. The principle cure is to square off the land and let the sides go wild. I suggest planting trees and wild flowers. Twice a year a rice blessing should be done. Throw handful of rice up in the air to feed the spirits of the Air. Throw handfuls of rice on the ground to feed the ground spirits that protect you. Acknowledge the good fortune they bring you all year long.

There are many shapes of land due to developers trying to maximize the land use and make it as profitable as possible. Each shape has its own opportunities for you to be creative.

You can e-mail me **fengshuing@bellsouth.net** and we can discuss your land choices and development concerns.

## 13

## YOUR POWER

Tired in the morning?

Can't sleep at night?

Wake up in the middle of the night and can't go back to sleep? Are you always tired?

Your personal energy is your power! The proper amount of sleep keeps your immune system in good order. Preserve your energy, get the proper rest, and eat a healthy diet.

**Heaven to Earth Energy Technique**

Stand by the side of the bed --- or against a wall if it makes you feel more balanced. Push your feet into the floor and put your arms over your head, palms facing the ceiling. You are now a pillar between Heaven and Earth.

The heavenly energy enters the top of your head, travels clockwise through your head, neck, chest, trunk, hands and arms of your body, down your legs into your feet, down to the center of the earth.

The energy of the earth is pulled back up through your feet, legs, trunk, hands, arms, neck, and through the top of your head, back to heaven. See the diagram and check the colors of each area. Do this three times a day.

Breathe to the count of six, inhale through your nose exhale, through the mouth.

Keep a calendar of the days you practice each suggested exercise and meditation.

# Memorize the colors of the chakras and their positions.

Pink - top of head charaka

Purple - crown charaka

Blue - throat charaka

Green -heart charaka

Yellow -solar plexus-charaka

Orange-stomach char aka

Red- root charaka

Inner Feng Shui for Health

Outer Feng Shui for Success

## *IMAGINE*

The top of your head is pink.

Between your eyes is purple.

Your throat area is blue.

Your heart area is green.

The solar plexus is yellow.

The stomach area is orange.

The root area is red.


If you can imagine these colors during your meditation it will help you concentrate.


I also imagine that there is a little door at each area and I open each door when I start the meditation and close the doors when I finish the meditation.

For example…The pink door opens at the top of my head.

The purple door opens in the middle of my eyes.

The blue door opens at my throat area.

The green door opens at my heart area.

The yellow door opens in the solar plexus area.

The orange door opens in the stomach area.

The red door opens in the sexual area.

If you are not asleep by this time, reverse the sequence and close the doors.

The red door closes.

The orange door closes.

The yellow door closes.

The green door closes.

The blue door closes.

The purple door closes.

The pink door closes.

        Good Night.


If you wake up during the night, just do the meditation again.

## 14

## WHEN LITTLE ACHES BOTHER YOU

Lay in bed on your back palms facing the ceiling, and say "E*nergy, energy, energy*." This draws the energy into your hands. Your hand will get hot and you transfer the heat to pressure point areas.

Cup your hands and place them on the crown of your head. Visualize the color Purple covering the top of your head. Breathe in through your nose, out through your mouth, and count to nine. Allow the heat of your hands to comfort the area.

Move your cupped hands down to cover your eyes, visualize the color navy Blue banding your eyes, breathe in through your nose, out through your mouth, count to nine. The heat of your hands will comfort the area.

Moved cupped hands down to your throat, circle the throat (do not touch your throat, your hands should be about one to two inches away from the skin) and visualize the color Turquoise. Do your breathing to the count of nine. Feel the heat of your hands comforting the area.

Move cupped hands to the heart area, span the chest area with your hands (again do not touch your chest, but keep your cupped hands about two inches away) visualize the color green circling your chest. Breathe to the count of nine. Feel the heat of your hands relaxing the heart.

Move cupped hands to the Solar Plexus; six inches above the navel (two inches away from the skin) see the color Yellow.

Breathe to the count of nine. Feel the heat of your hands warming the Liver, Gall Bladder, and Spleen, relaxing them.

Move cupped hands to span the Stomach (two inches away from the skin) and visualize the color Orange. Breathe to the count of nine. Feel the heat relax the stomach and help digestion.

Move cupped hands to span the sexual organs, (two inches away from the skin) and visualize the color Red. Breathe to the count of nine. A chiropractor told me that if you relaxed the groin muscles, sleep would come quickly.

When your hands are cupped they need space away from the skin to transfer the heat that comes into your hands.

Are you still a wake?

All the points are open, so let's use the close the door visualization again.

*Feng Shui Secrets...*

Visualize, a red door in your sexual region. It is open. Let's close the red door. You are shutting the red door. You feel more relaxed. Your hands warm the area.

Visualize, an orange door. It is open. Let's close the orange door. You are shutting the orange door. You feel the warmth of your hands relaxing the stomach.

Visualize, a yellow door at the Solar Plexus, close the yellow door. The warmth of your hands relaxes the inner organs.

Visualize, a green door at the Heart. The door is open. Let's close the green door. The Heart muscle feel very relaxed.

Visualize, a blue door at the throat. The door is open. Let's close the blue door. The throat is relaxed, and the warmth of your hands is soothing to your throat.

Visualize, a purple door at the space between your eyes. The door is open. Let's close the blue door. Your warm hands relax the eyes you are so relaxed and sleepy.

Visualize, a pink door at the top of your head. The door is open. Let's close the pink door. The warm hands on the top of your head feel comforting.

<u>You should do this exercise three times</u>. When you finish, yawn 3 times, and go to sleep. Good Night!

## 13

# CHINESE ASTROLOGY ANIMALS & COLORS

**Black**
**Rat**     2020  2008  1996  1984
            1972  1960  1948  1936

**Turquoise**
**Ox**      2021  2009  1997  1985
            1973  1961  1949  1937

**Dog**     2022  2010  1998  1986
            1974  1962  1950  1938

**Green**
**Rabbit**  2023  2011  1999  1987
            1975  1963  1951  1939

**Purple**
**Dragon**  2024  2012  2000  1988
            1976  1964  1952  1940

**Snake**   2025  2013  2001  1989
            1977  1965  1953  1941

**Red**
**Horse**   2026  2014  2002  1990
            1978  1966  1954  1942

**Pink**
**Ram**     2027  2015  2003  1991
            1979  1967  1955  1943

**Monkey**  2028  2016  2004  1992
            1980  1968  1956  1944

**White**
**Rooster**   2029  2017  2005  1993
              1981  1969  1957  1945

Write down your Astrological animal.

Write down your Astrological color.

Where does that fall on the Energy Chart?

Make a note of that area.

## About the Author

Nadine Gross is a graduate of the Metropolitan School of Interior Design, The Open Center of Professional Feng Shui Masters, Cooper Union, and New York University.

Her worldwide client base includes both residential and commercial clients.

## Professional Affiliations:
American Society of Interior Decorators (ASID)
American Institute of Interior Design (AID)
The American Federation of Astrologers (AFA)
The Fashion Group
The International Feng Shui Guild
The Cooper Union Alumni Association
Color Marketing Group

For information about Nadine's services, please visit…

www.FengShuiofSouthFlorida.com

www.Astrologyandfengshui.net

www.OwnYourSpaces.com

www.youtube.com/ownyourspaces

www.ReikiOfSouthFlorida.com


To book Nadine to speak to your group, at your event, or for Feng Shui design & energy consultation, please call (516)965-0144

Made in United States
Orlando, FL
27 June 2024